the Garfield Gallery 7

Jim Davis

RAVETTE BOOKS

First published by Ravette Books Limited 1991

Printed and bound for Ravette Books Limited
3 Glenside Estate, Star Road,
Partridge Green, Nr. Horsham,
West Sussex RH13 8RA
An Egmont Company
by STIGE, Italy

ISBN 1 85304 370 2

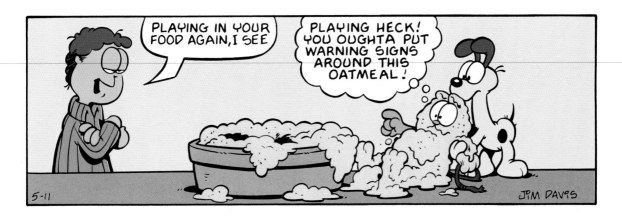

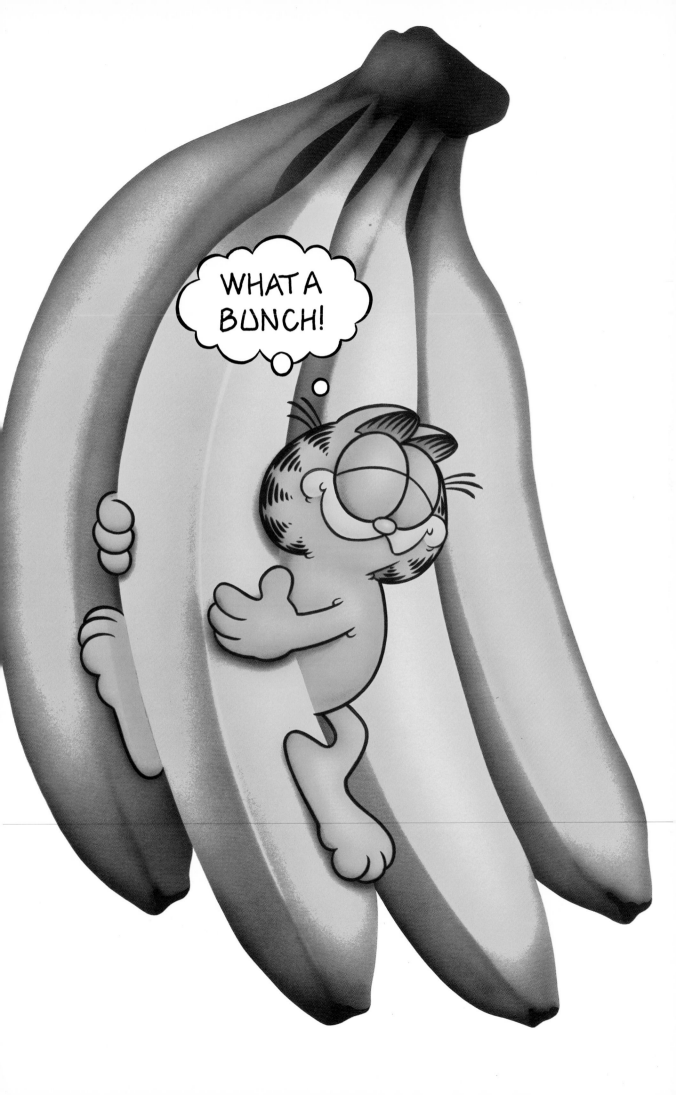

GOOD EVENING. THIS IS LANCE STERLING, YOUR MAN ON THE STREET

HERE COMES SOMEONE DOWN THE STREET NOW... MA'AM, WHICH ARE SMARTER, CATS OR DOGS?

WHY, CATS, OF COURSE

SMACK!

AND WHAT DO YOU THINK, SIR?

I THINK DOGS ARE SMARTER

POKE

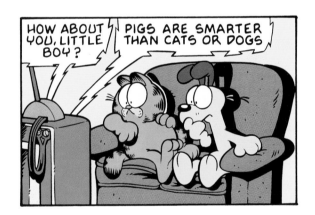

HOW ABOUT YOU, LITTLE BOY?

PIGS ARE SMARTER THAN CATS OR DOGS

PIGS ARE SMARTER THAN WE ARE? THAT'S HARD TO ACCEPT

© 1986 United Feature Syndicate, Inc.

COME ON, ODIE. LET'S GO DISCUSS THIS OVER A HAM SANDWICH

JIM DAVIS 6-1

© 1986 United Feature Syndicate, Inc.

SIGH

I'M BORED. THERE'S GOTTA BE SOMETHING TO DO

PETS ALWAYS SEEM TO BE ABLE TO ENTERTAIN THEMSELVES. MAYBE I COULD DO WHAT THEY DO

© 1986 United Feature Syndicate, Inc.

SO...PLAYED WITH ANY GOOD YARN LATELY?

JIM DAVIS 7-20

I GOT IT! I GOT IT!

CALL THE FUNNY FARM, REBA! ARBUCKLE'S FINALLY GONE OFF THE DEEP END!

ROWR

YIP! YIP!

BARK! BARK!

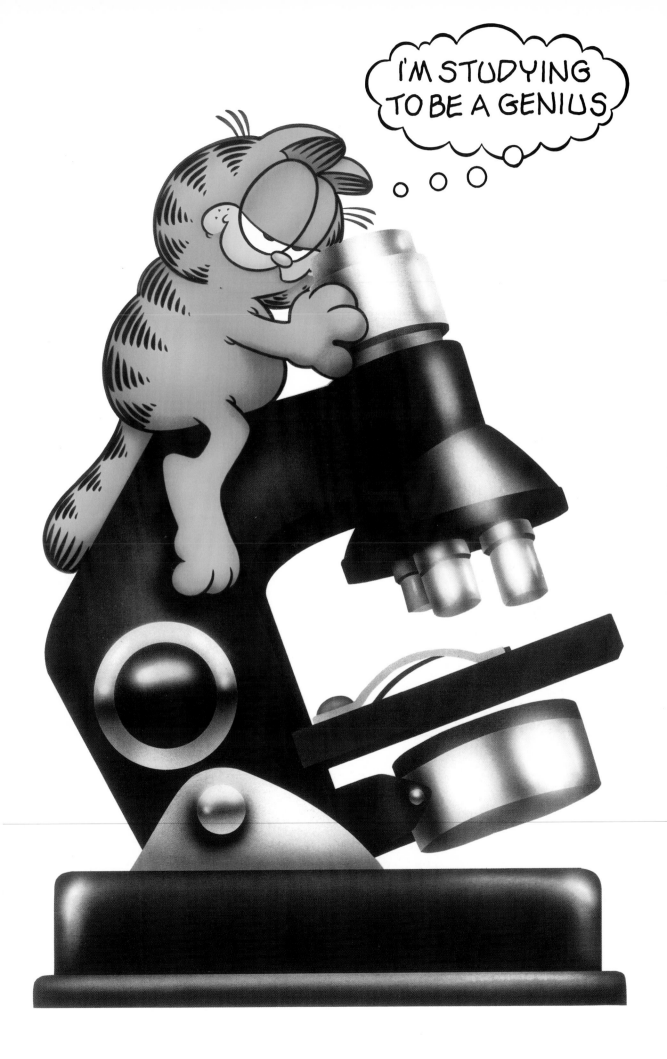

JIM DAVIS 8-3

© 1986 United Feature Syndicate, Inc.

JIM DAVIS 8-24

BEEP
BEEP
BIP
BOOP

HELLO? LOST AND FOUND? TAKE THIS DOWN. "MISSING: MY TWO PRECIOUS PETS ANSWERING TO THE NAMES 'GARFIELD' AND 'ODIE'. WHEN FOUND, CONTACT JON ARBUCKLE, 711 MAPLE STREET. LARGE REWARD. REPEAT, **LARGE** REWARD."

THAT "LARGE REWARD" BIT WILL HAVE EVERYBODY LOOKING

CLICK

© 1986 United Feature Syndicate, Inc.

THE NEXT DAY...

AH! THERE'S MY AD. JON BOY, YOU THOUGHT OF EVERYTHING

DING DONG ♫

I WONDER WHO THAT COULD BE?

JIM DAVIS 8-31

WHOA, SIMBA! ER I MEAN, ODIE

I FOUND GARFIELD AND ODIE, MITHTER

MAYBE I SHOULD HAVE BEEN MORE SPECIFIC

HELLO, DOGGIE.
ARE YOU LOST?

JIM DAVIS 9-7

WOULD YOU LIKE TO
COME HOME WITH ME?

© 1986 United Feature Syndicate, Inc.

HMMM

AND HOW WOULD YOU LIKE THOSE
SILLY EARS OF YOURS TIED
IN A SQUARE KNOT?

I THOUGHT SO

© 1986 United Feature Syndicate, Inc.   JiM DAViS 9-21

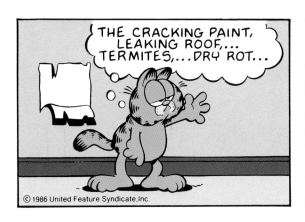

© 1986 United Feature Syndicate, Inc.

9-28

JIM DAVIS

© 1986 United Feature Syndicate,Inc.

JiM DAViS 10-12

SLUUUCK

© 1986 United Feature Syndicate, Inc.

SPLOOSH!

I ASSUME THERE'S A REASON FOR THIS

I'D LIKE TO GET YOUR ASSESSMENT OF THE POSSIBILITY OF BLUEBERRY PANCAKES FOR BREAKFAST

© 1986 United Feature Syndicate, Inc.

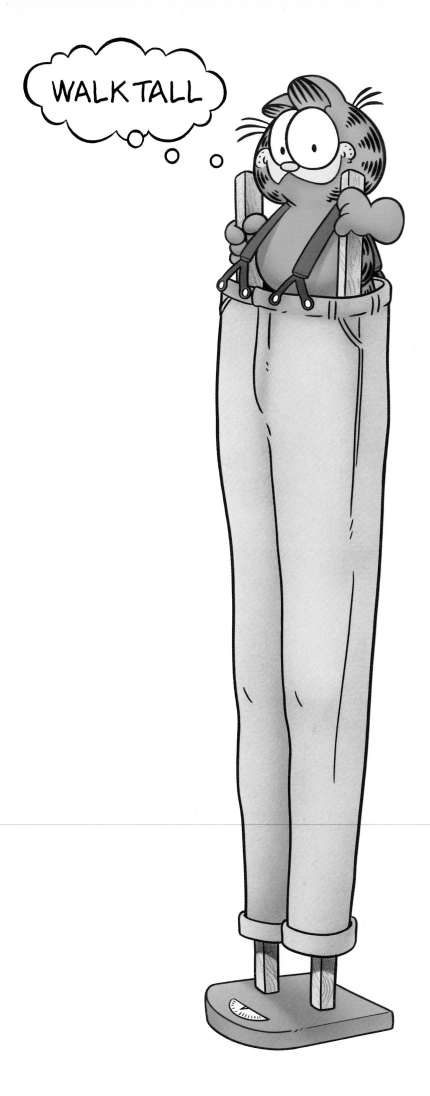

© 1986 United Feature Syndicate, Inc.

JIM DAVIS 12-7

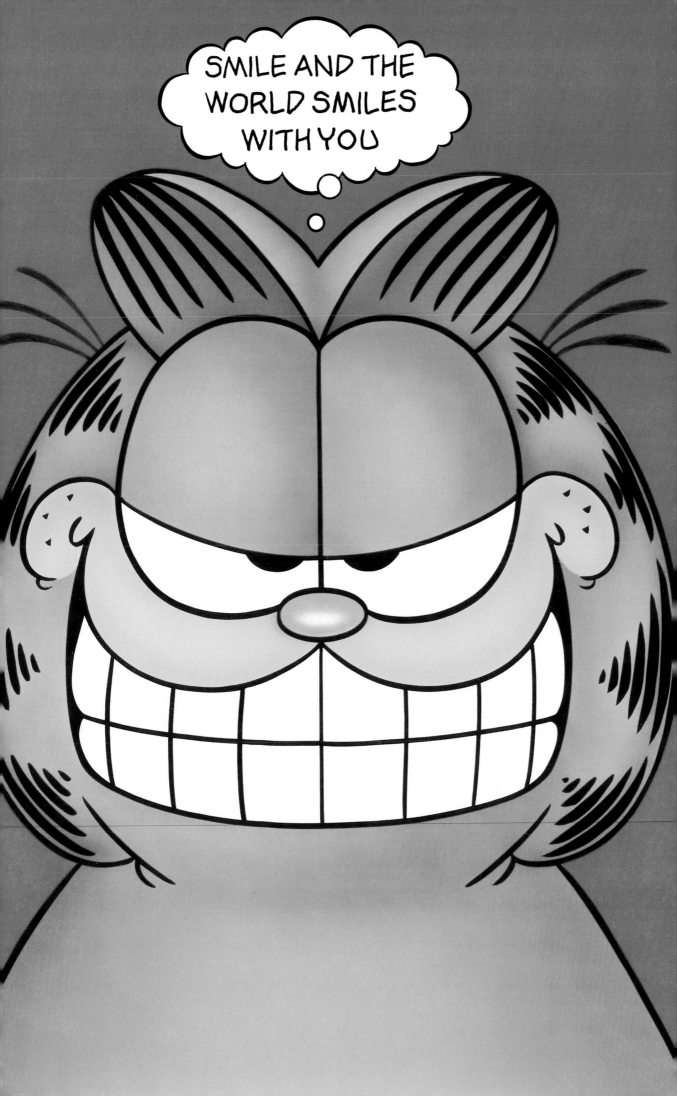

© 1987 United Feature Syndicate, Inc.

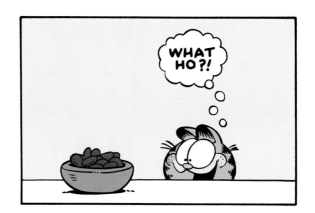

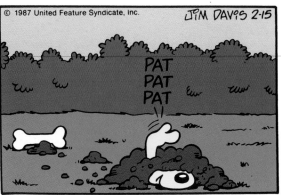

© 1987 United Feature Syndicate, Inc.

JIM DAVIS 2-15

IT'S ONE OF THOSE MORNINGS

THE KIND OF MORNING WHERE YOU'VE BEEN UP FOR TWO MINUTES AND IT FEELS LIKE TWO DAYS

IF I CAN JUST MAKE IT TO MY COFFEE, I'LL BE ALL RIGHT

JIM DAVIS 2-22

IT'S IN SIGHT! COME ON, GARFIELD! YOU CAN MAKE IT!

WHUMP!

SO CLOSE, AND YET SO FAR

Z